The Beast Inside

Bill Cushing

Southern
Arizona
Press

Southern Arizona Press
Sierra Vista, Arizona

The Beast Inside

By Bill Cushing

First Edition

Content Copyright © 2025 by Bill Cushing

Author: Bill Cushing
Editor: Paul Gilliland
Formatting: Southern Arizona Press
Cover Art: "The Brute in the Brain," sketch by Winslow McCay, c.1920

Published by Southern Arizona Press
Sierra Vista, Arizona 85635
www.SouthernArizonaPress.com

ISBN: 978-1-960038-58-6

Poetry

The Beast Inside
Bill Cushing

With thanks to the "usual suspects" who help in making my work look better than it might by way of the multiple workshops and writing sessions they welcome me into: Don Kingfisher Campbell, Gabriela Docan, Robin Dunn, Alex Frankel, Lenora Good, Andria Hill, and William Slattery.

Thanks also to my preview readers, John Brantingham, Emily Robin Clark, and Linda Imbler.

Foreword

I was delighted and quite honored to be asked by Poet Bill Cushing to write the foreword to what will soon be one of his most popular poetry collections. As a fellow poet, Bill's work has always resonated with me. It's thrilling that he is adding this new set of verse to his publications. All who have followed his work over the years, and new readers who will discover his talent through the medium of this new volume, will find their yearning for fine poetry fulfilled.

While reading through the manuscript, I was reminded of a powerful quotation about poetry penned by the enigmatic Edgar Allen Poe. Poe wrote "If a poem hasn't ripped apart your soul, then you haven't experienced poetry."

Trust me, there's a superabundance of ripping to be experienced within these pages.

You will discover this for yourself as you read through this stunning compilation. For within the framework of "self," this book is first and foremost a treasury of love poems—for family, friends, people Cushing has never met yet admires, and reactions to places and events. Mr. Cushing, as a miner of exquisite poetical skill, you have once again struck gold.

Linda Imbler
February, 2025

Introduction

Since ancient Greece, when Socrates likely advised us to "know thyself," humans have been obsessed with the notion of self in many ways—as a soul, as an essence, as either conscious or subconscious, or as a singular self versus a collection of selves.

At the very least we are creatures of duality however one categorizes it. It may be a duality of primitive versus civilized, the duality of individuality or tribalism, the duality of conscious versus unconscious (with subconscious thrown in for good measure).

The list of supposition seems endless, which helped bring me to *The Beast Inside*.

This book was inspired in more ways than one by Winslow McCaw's early 20th century sketch, a piece I encountered as an ekphrastic writing exercise. That final poem in this work led me back to his drawing over and over again. From there, it isn't a great leap to explain how I wanted to organize the writings in this volume.

While the notion of self and the number possible is interesting, as a writer, I'm a big believer in the "rule of threes," namely that humans love seeing things organized around that particular prime number. After all, we tend to see one as an accident and two as coincidence. Once we have a third category (or whatever descriptor is chosen), it appears to establish a pattern.

And if there's one thing we love, it's patterns.

With that in mind, allow me to decipher the three "selves" I conceived for these pages. I've named them in order of appearance: reminiscent, formal, and dream-state.

How did I decide on those names—or "selves?" Like most rule of three scenarios, it was pretty simple (or "basic" might be the better term).

The "reminiscent" self recalls events, people, moments whether personal or historical. The "formal" self follows directions. In my case, this section collects some of the poetic formats I've been getting involved with over recent years, which has been an interesting and fun exercise in discipline. Finally, the "dream-state" self conjures images, be they dreams, imaginings, or tangents off of reality.

So, there you have it. I hope that, in reading this book, you might meet some of your own "selves." Certainly, you'll encounter mine.

Contents

THE REMINISCENT SELF

THE FORMAL SELF

THE DREAM-STATE SELF

THE REMINISCENT SELF
Remembrances, recollections, and reflections from life

AT MRS. GANNETT'S

In a tidy house cluttered with kindness,
surrounded by her late husband's bric-a-brac,
she showed us his walking stick
that doubled as a scabbard hiding a blade.

We local kids would sit, encircling her,
and eat candy from a pink crystal dish
as she delighted us with stories
of her childhood in Omaha.

It was the only time I saw a bike horn
mounted on a wheelchair. She preferred candles,
disdained lightbulbs. This made her
invulnerable to the '65 blackout.

I picture her now, couched on some celestial
divan, and wonder if she ever got her wish
to return upstairs before
she was laid to rest in Zion's church grounds.

First appeared in *Steps: Four Feathers*

BOSCH DREAMS

Like the spilling of fading photos,
images from a life spent in isolation
cascade to hone his own fixation.
Memory fractures his attempts

to escape reality, and wanting
from all the wanting,
he grasps need in every grey day
trying to reach a lull from life.

With a mind dulled,
his hand and stomach quiver,
waiting on the needle and vial,
seeking the spell of denial.

His only price of admission
being guilt, for like the false vows
and promises of any politician,
his addiction never intends

to deliver a real solution.
Reality upends the high,
to become a machete slicing
through his life as through meat.

First appeared in *Poet-Tree Imagazine*

ADIÓS PUERTORRIQUEÑOS

The enigma of a plebescite:
commonwealth or state?
Embracing statehood would ablate
cultural roots, which would take flight.
Such a vote would act as last rites.

Its people will lose, inevitably,
the indigenous soul of *Taino*,
and then *isla del encanto*
becomes another Disney.
Just ask Hawaii.

First place award for Geographic Place, 2025 Highland Park
Poetry Challenge

AN UNLIKELY LOOKING ACE
(R.I.P. October 22, 2024)

He looked more like an auto mechanic
or a short-order cook yet could also

have been Diego Rivera's son. Squat with
a slight pudge, *el Toro* bore the lineage

of the *Yoreme*, became one to don Dodger blue,
then carved his name into the game so securely

that even those not familiar with the game
have heard the word "Fernandomania."

First appeared in *Bardball*

FIGHTING THE HAWK IN RED HOOK, 1983

My worst day at ship's work?
Had to be that February in Brooklyn when
I met the hawk, arctic blasts that went berserk
as my mate and I tried to pry loose
bolts holding a motor to the deck's windlass.

The wind's hawk tore talons through
our clothes, no matter how many layers we wore.
Our hands chapped, our ears frozen,
we couldn't last more than five-minutes,
forced to retreat into interior shelter.

Once, glancing west past the tip
of Governor's Island while in that icy grip,
I could see Lady Liberty
standing her post, but I'm pretty sure
she too shivered from that gusting hawk.

AT THE STATIONERS

Wearing a blue-and-white striped apron, meaty hands resting
on hips, Mrs. Bernstein was as close to a babushka
as suburban Queens got. She stood guard at a freezer
filled with ice cream cups and wooden spoons whose aftertaste
stayed way past the frozen flavor. She surveilled boys
surveying the rows of plastic models in boxes
layered with dust that disbursed into a million motes when moved.

At the other end of the corner building, dimly lit
by flickering fluorescent tubes, cluttered
corridors of shelves sat, spilling sundries: yellow tubes
of airplane glue, boxes of Crayolas, and marbled
notebooks that ended in a wood-and-glass counter
filled with rows of Turkish taffy, paper-wrapped squares
of Bazooka bubble gum, wax lips, and Pez dispensers.

Her husband stands, his pear of a body in grey trousers;
strands of hair crossing his balding head. He'd chew his cigar,
eternally unlit, while his look disdained the row of bikes
propped against his storefront window. Then, scowling
at the kids from the school up the street who leafed through
dime comics, he'd bark his ever-reliable mantra:
"Come on, come on! This ain't no library."

First appeared in *Remember When*

RESURRECTION OF PONCE

The push of volcanic eruptions
created this fabric of rocky land between
ocean and the Caribbean, its people now jarred
by shifting plates of earth, being battered
after so much damage, first Hugo,
then Maria, now Ian.

The stress of collapsed buildings rattled
the people, broken yet undefeated,
who will reach back to their indigenous
Taino roots. Ponce, cradle of native art,
will rise from rubble,
return to Isla del Encanto.

GREETING THE NEXT DAY

As my son sleeps, I see my father.
The child exhales, and nascent breath flows
across my hand. I stroke his hair;

sometimes I stand there, propping
my hands on the posts of the bed
to watch him breathe, witness his growth.

I cannot see it but know it is happening,
and at certain intervals—a day or days,
sometimes months, I can perceive it.

Today I couldn't help but note
how much bigger his hands have become,
with fingers I have had wrapped

around my own. He slips from sleep
and becomes aware of my presence.
He brushes open drowsy eyes.

CRESCENDO

It is said when
on his death bed,
Beethoven lifted
his lion-maned head,
propped himself on joints
weakened by age,
and though
unable to hear
the thunder
rattling the casements
of those windowpanes,
shook his fists
and pointed at the sky,
glaring at the lightning outside
as if to chide God and His angels
to beware, for they were about to bear
witness to a new,
unhumbled essence —
and they
would hear him
express an eternal note—
bold and relentless
filled with the rumbling of kettle drums,
a blare of brass.

First appeared in *Ink Nest*

CARING FOR A CRIPPLE

"Don't use that term,"
they demand, these people
who wince at my language,
but I refuse to indulge
in denial of my son's infirmities.
He is indeed crippled
inside and out,
so I wince as well
and shudder
at their clumsy attempts
as they try to understand,
even sympathize.
I know they mean well.

But when I reckon "Everything
happens for a reason,"
which is true,

or "You must advocate
for your child,"
my inner voice replies,

"Yes, but the reason is medical,
not spiritual or otherworldly."

"I am not my child's advocate
I'm his honey badger."

THROWING WORDS

Is it true that the villagers in Salem
burned the first female ventriloquist at the stake
for mesmeric witchcraft?

"The beauty of it all," he says from across the room
through a candlestick, "is this: Every insult, any slight,
reproach or flirtation is never my fault."

She answers using his coffee cup, "I love that this art
allows me to find my way to being anyone
or anything else other than myself."

But the real idol, the true icon of ventriloquism
has to be Cardi B, so skilled she was able
to throw her voice and her mic at the same time.

First appeared in *Line of Poetry*

TO GABRIEL, REFLECTING ON YOUR FIRST YEAR

You open your eyes to look out at a world
but cannot see what is in store.

As soldiers attacked Iraq,
your first tooth arrived—late.

You battled weak muscles, twisted joints
while people turned planes into bombs:

acts not your fault but will be
your peers' ever-after problem.

One could round off your life
to these first 52 weeks, enough time to make

each day full, complete. For me, the effort
has proved a delightful duty.

FAMILIAL TIES

They share the innocence that comes
from the purity of damaged brains.
He never met his favorite aunt yet
always went to her picture to stare. Seated
in my deceased sister's chair, my son,
muted by blood that clotted in his head,

would lean into his crooked hand,
creating a contemplative pose.
What thoughts crossed his mind
as he watched videos and heard
Bob the Builder ask, "Can we fix it?"
I wonder: did he think, *Yes, we can!*

First appeared in *Keeping the Flame Alive*

LIVING IN A FEEDBACK LOOP

Talk is haphazard: we miss
each other's bandwidth
as if, frequently, our
frequencies try to
connect, but I hear cross
modulations. Perhaps it's all
static. I hear sound in the
distance: Bugs Bunny and Yosemite Sam
garble back-and-forth insults
while Joe Cocker gets "high
with a little help from my friends."
My son repeats these five-
second bursts of attention
that then repeat themselves

First appeared in *Locust Shells Journal*

THE CRUELTY OF LIFE

Which is the crueler of tricks
mortality has in store:
Preparation and foreknowledge,
or blinding ignorance shaking
confidence to the core?

Through teary eyes, a woman
cleans the hose feeding her father's
breath. He won't be much longer,
yet she helps him cling to life,
putting her own on hold.

On New Year's Eve, a doctor
celebrates the fleeting year
at a party, unaware
she will bring in the annum
pronouncing the death of her son.

Another family gathers about a son
to celebrate his birth.
The next day they prepare
his grandmother's remains
for her return as earth.

FALLEN MIGHTY

Once her beauty could pry
others' eyes from a bride.

Then, she was forced to swallow
the pill of becoming human

as obligations, and her life
as a wife, tore down her facade,

stripping the illusion
of cosmetics to reveal

the person below the surface,
the one who was real.

First appeared in *Poet-Tree Imagazine*

UNVARNISHED TRUTHS

A boy, playing in the attic, discovers
a crawl space just tall enough for him to stand.
He trains his father's flashlight at an unexplored
corner, sees the shine from a loop of metal
links that hang from the rafter to the floor,
bolted into the wooden beam above him.

Later, playing with his sister, a girl
hobbled and yoked to her own mental constraints,
he recalls those interlocked ovals
of steel. He asks his mother about the chains,
why they are there. She stammers an answer,
something about it being there when they moved in.

At 18, he ships out with the Navy, climbs
the attic stairs to store belongings there,
to free his bedroom for one of his young
sisters. Again, he sees those looping fetters
secured to the collar. Again, he asks, "Why
are those chains still upstairs?" Then, he learns how,

a century before, when the house was built,
that family's child, much like his sister,
brain-damaged, trammeled, different from others.
Perhaps it was fear; more than likely it was
the ways of their times. Their solution: Leave her
in that crawl space, shackled to one corner.

That way, she would not hurt herself or others;
that way, they need not confront realities.
Either way, his parents left those linked
reminders where they were. That way, his parents
knew they'd freed themselves from the chains
of past ills, practices of discarded thought.

First appeared in *Last Stanza*

A PERFECT MOMENT

Plans are set, and obligations are meant
to be met, but sometimes—not often,
but sometimes,
standing in a combination
of hot and cold that is so right, so perfect,

every attempt to close the spigots
and shut off the steaming
stream of water in the shower
gets interrupted by the thought:
"Not just yet."

First appeared in *Glomag*

IMAGES ON THE SPECTRUM

It's not out of place to see him
clap his hands over ears inside
a moving bus,
but then he sits, placid and
passive, singing children's tunes while
fire, police, or ambulance sirens wail past.

Then there are my questions. Is
the itsy-bitsy spider
really Sisyphus—
always starting over?
Does my child grasp my hand to make
human contact or prevent the hug he knows will come?

REFLECTIONS ON A WRITING
WORKSHOP

Thirty poets congregate, gathering
in the shade of the hosts' backyard beneath
lemons that dangle like dimpled
organic Christmas decorations.

We receive instructions: "Take seven minutes
and produce a poem"—as if spontaneity
comes from a faucet. "Write a poem a day," we're told.
"Poems are found everywhere," which may be true,

but I don't find a poem. It finds me. Then,
the reading. Burning coals of devotion,
readers deliver observations, thoughts, or
emotions—each in their own way.

Words spill as each mouth tries
to draw interest from the others or
at least exact a measure of masochism.
Some fly. Others stumble or wander from the trail.

Some rap. Some sermonize.
A few make the effort to memorize
what they have extracted from themselves.
"Take your iPhones and throw them in the lake,"

admonishes one who reads
from the screen of a laptop. Another
participant offers a page with text
and arrows—as if a poem is a flow chart.

An aging dog ambles, moving one lap
to the next, looks for food or scratches
under the chin from any benevolent guest.
Sated, he rests his head on crossed front paws.

VENN DIAGRAMS UNBURDENED BY
WHAT HAS BEEN

It's part of a nostalgia and memory
that the school bus takes us there, where it's time

for us to do what we have been doing,
and that time is every day. You need to get to go

and need to be able to get where you need to go
to do the work, for who

doesn't love a yellow school bus?
When we speak of the children of the community,

they are the children of the community.
What can be unburdened by what has been?

It's part of the experience of growing up;
when you think about it,

the significance of the passage of time
is of great significance to the passage of time.

Every day is time for us to agree
to slow this thing down. Every moment in time

we need to see the moment in time
in which we exist and are present

and contextualize it to where we exist
in the history and the moment as it relates

not only to the past but to the future.
Think of this moment as a moment

about great momentum but inspired by—also—
our collective ability to see what has been

unburdened by what will be.
Everything is in context;

you exist in context of all
in which you lived and what came before you.

WHAT JADE LEARNED FROM KATRINA

She came from a coddled city
that sat in Dionysian comfort,
secure in the superiority
of human endeavor. Enter Nature

to deliver its own brutal parade
as water waltzed in, flooding bars
and open-air markets, sloshing
around, up to second stories. After,

Jade huddled with others in stadium seats
under the threadbare quilt of hope
and fake security, joining thousands
waiting for an incompetent state

to attend to the problem when,
in the end, she watched soldiers,
under orders to shoot
in order to keep the peace.

THE NEWEST IMPALER

Your mother seemed
to have chosen well
when she deemed
you go through life
known as Vlad, a man
whose story is not
unlike your own.

Now you try to tear
the world apart
and reconstruct
the empire of czars.
Instead, you united most nations
but not under your thumb
as planned.

Even the Swedes and Finns,
notoriously neutral,
seek protection
from your ambitions.
The images we see
display your violence,
violation, and envy.

Vladimir, defiled and filled
with the hope
of reviving an empire
into existence,
descends into violence
presenting a pretense
of deliverance.

First appeared in *Fine Lines*

THREE CATS

- kitten -
A tail twitches
from behind a skate
laid on its side
in a closet.
Worn and hard rubber wheels
face out so that each time
the kitten passes,
rubbing an arched back
against them, they move,
scraping protests
out from mottled rust,
of memories past

- watch cat -
The sentry walks the night,
on cat feet that assert
his territory. He ricochets
in a clumsy
and meandering way
against a stucco wall,
keeping one eye
(his only one)
on the grounds
as he makes rounds.

-feral cat -
It took months
and bribes stolen
from the kitchen,
but eventually,
he took to me,
sitting in my lap
while I napped,
waiting for the day shift.

When they arrive,
their footsteps scare him
again, every time,
and he scurries, fleeing
under the building's boilers
to wait for the next
midnight.

First appeared in *Odd or Even*

RE: JOYCE

It was in my thirtieth year
that I met an ebony
woman of primal beauty
and supple elegance,
dancing an angelic arabesque
whose hands reached to touch,
and in touching embrace,
moved me to a place
of serenity,
giving me the ability
to ignore life's pallor
and bathed me,
if only for that year,
with nothing less than joy.

First appeared in *Rejoice or Rue*

THE FORMAL SELF
Poems that follow certain rules

42 WORDS

The following pieces first appeared in *Book of 42²*, a 2024 anthology of 42 42-word submissions divided into 42 categories. Also, each title consists of 42 characters.

Because the publisher wanted a different name for each entry, the *nom de plume* has been provided where needed.

FORTY-TWO WORDS REGARDING THE GREATEST #42

Jackie Robinson enlisted in '42 and was commissioned—
unsurprising given all he'd done, even beyond sports.
With commanding character and dignity,
following a year in the Negro Leagues, he shattered
a massive barrier. Ever after, the number 42
became his personal territory.

Appeared under my real name

GUARIONEX'S DESCENDANTS DO THEIR JOB RIGHT

When Spain's conquistadors landed in Puerto Rico,
the *Taino* saw them as invincible gods. Then,
three natives spotted a lone soldier at a river.
Using the scientific method,
they overpowered and drowned him,
letting them know
the time to rebel was right.

Appeared under the name "Fajardo Resident"

THE MEANING OF LIFE TOLD IN FORTY-TWO WORDS

"What is the meaning of life?"
Grasshopper asks the Master.
The ancient one then recounts one's daily routine:
walking, urinating, eating, bathing,
along with all the things we do
to keep our bodies operating. Then, he tells his student,
"Life is maintenance."

Appeared under the name "The Craw"

WHILE IN MY DAD'S HOUSE, AFTER HIS FUNERAL

Sifting through his clothes, I pull a jacket
from the closet, turn toward a mirror, and see
gray hair and beard, but
the child gets swallowed in its shoulders
while the cuffs brush knuckles. Blushing,
I return it to its rightful place.

Appeared under the name Peter Grant

The remaining pieces of this section adhere to established poetic forms as listed below.
In the case of unusual categories, a "primer" of sorts has been provided:

1. Cinquain
2. Dodoitsu (a Japanese quatrain of three seven-syllable lines followed by a five-syllable line, usually acting as a sort of "punchline" for the piece)
3. Ghazal
4. Haibun (a short prose-poetic piece followed by a haiku as summary)
5. Haiku
6. Imayo (yet more Japanese poetic forms, these are four lines of two sections each—the first part being seven syllables, the second being five syllables; the trick is to make the whole piece work as a whole while also creating a poem where the four seven-syllable lines can be read as a separate piece, and the same can be done with the four five-syllable lines)
7. Ode (the first also being a cento, where the writer incorporates quotes from other sources and pieces them together as a whole; in this case, I am using pieces of Vienna Teng's lyrics and titles)
8. Ovillejo (a Spanish form that follows a rhyme scheme and set syllable count where the second, fourth, and sixth lines are used to create a final statement)
9. Villanelle
10. Senryu (like a haiku but more satirical or humorous instead of focusing its theme on nature)
11. Sijo
12. Sonnet
13. Concrete poem

A MEMORIAL CINQUAIN

Ana,
a palindrome:
your affection for art
guided us to a place we could
call love.

GENETICALLY TWISTED CINQUAIN

Be who you
are. When your woes
double—you can still dive
deep, playing music to derive
three rows.

First appeared in *Poet-Tree Imagazine*

DODOITSU FOR SAYAH ESMA

She is our well-born female,
born God's exalted cargo,
adored and blessèd shadow
whose *canto* prevails.

First appeared in *Glomag*

GRIEF RELEASED (a ghazal)

The more I live, the greater the grief;
the best I can do is treasure the grief.

I began life with promise, but found
that life can only guarantee grief.

Improvising the normal along with
remorse allows me to see grief.

If not relief, let me regain the mundane;
I only ask that you leave me, grief.

Moving on is a slow pained process,
the only avenue to flee grief.

The more resilient I can become,
the better I can set free grief.

The best way to pay the bill is to dive
into the human element, and leave me grief.

First appeared in *Four Feathers*

HAPPY BOTTOM HAIBUN

Florence Lowe dropped from the clouds to buzz the California church where she'd married the good and modest Reverend Barnes. That church still stands, signifying her family's failed attempt to make her respectable. Before taking to the sky, Florence lived just as interesting a life. She ran guns to Mexico in 1920, taking the name Pancho after using a bandana to create "the best-lookin' balls" on the boat. Pancho Barnes was born, and like any great sailor, her profanity could blister ears. She exchanged perfume and silk for oil and leather to become "one of the greatest pilots that ever wore pants." She flew faster than Amelia Earhardt. As opposed to the model good looks of Earhardt, Pancho was what they called "one tough broad," beating up a Hollywood mogul who attested her bathtub gin was "the best." She became Hollywood's first stunt pilot and filled in as a horse rider for Louise Fazenda, a Hollywood star who couldn't look less like Pancho, described as "uglier than a hornet" and just as brazen.

Once back on the ground, she opened a bar in Muroc, where testosterone mixed with heat and fumes before the place became Edwards Air Force Base. Naming her building the Happy Bottom Riding Club, she drank with the likes of Jimmy Doolittle and Chuck Yeager, spending time "high in the sky in the day; high in the bars at night." Betrayed by the Air Force, she sued and won. Her refusal to submit to government wishes put her on J Edgar Hoover's shit list. Perhaps the best shrine for Pancho Barnes isn't that Pasadena church where she began her independence but the charred walls that remain of the Happy Bottom Riding Club, destroyed by a mysterious fire.

While she never flew
with proper society
she earned her respect

First appeared in *Line of Poetry*

A HAIBUN FOR GUNNER'S MATE
STYLES

Joe Styles never made it to high school, tilling his dad's land instead. Then, he heard—and heeded—the call of a still-patriotic nation. Ceding farm-calloused hands to sea, he boarded tin cans for Korea, stayed until Vietnam. Immersed in munitions, he maintained, calibrated, and fed weapons from 50-cals to five-inchers, even Alpha and anti-submarine rockets—blunt-nosed bombs that traveled miles.
With a cigarette in one hand, in the other a broken-in ceramic mug—at the ready and emblazoned with crossed cannons, he'd squint as if to contemplate tangents, azimuths, windage, elevation. Showing the smarts and steady skill to deliver the killing blow, he climbed the ranks to become Chief Styles. Comfortable in khakis but stiff in dress blues. He punctuated life with insight of his own: "Never trust a man whose wardrobe includes loafers but no socks."

his eyes pierced a line
with sight more true than the times
he'd bleed saltwater

First appeared in *Atlantean Journal*

ETERNAL HAIKU

As world leaders
dance a martial minuet
we waltz into war

First appeared in *Failed Haiku*

HAIKU ON DEATH

I have accepted
old age, even my life's end,
but what happens next?

First appeared in *Bamboo Hut*

OWL HAIKU

Hidden in a tree,
three grey owls, birds of prey, wait
for their hour to hunt.

First appeared in *The Bamboo Hut*

A SLINKY IMAYO

With only one moving part, it gave us hours of
entertainment in our youth— joy in our childhood.
Using its torsional spring, arching down the steps,
a spiral circle moving—in shaky stasis.

First appeared in *Toys: Four Feathers*

HIROMI'S IMAYO

Playing like a mad hatter, Hiromi performs
glissando from Bach to blues, connects then to now.
Her face flaunts infectious fun—reflected in chords
through the music in her bones, transferred to the keys.

First appeared in *Writing World: World Music Day*

IMAYO FOR THE SOLOIST

Fluid fingers sprint across, sharing her love of
Tchaikovsky's concerto and, throwing her hair back,
untethers joy's energy. Even in tacit,
we listeners sit, in awe, enthusiastic.

First appeared in *Startled by Music*

SUB-IMAYO: USS Tang, Pacific Theater*

Bubbles guide us through the seas, hidden under waves:
death less than an inch away—until battle's done.
We climb ladders to clean air, and we've beaten back
enemy surface vessels—our adversaries.

First appeared in *Poet-Tree Imagazine*

* During World War II, the USS Tang sank 33 enemy vessels
to become the deadliest submarine in the Navy at that time.
Ironically, the Tang was sunk by its own torpedo in the Taiwan
Strait in 1944

UNCHECKED BAGGAGE

We lance our festering boils—spurting toxic pus,
fixed and buried derision, with poisoned disdain
passing for conversation, we share old tantrums—
what is really cradled weight—and our martyrdom.

First appeared in *Line of Poetry*

CENTO ODE TO VIENNA

Dreaming through the noise in a place named for deities
where great musicians can feel a homecoming
while at the center of communal economies
between the Alps and the Vienna basin.
This city of music that sits off the Danube,
its name affixed to a forest stream,
sings a hymn for axiom. A lullaby for a stormy night
proves enough to go by but nothing without you.
Level up to whatever you want to dream;
just never look away from the breaking light.

ODE TO OTYKEN

They named themselves for the middle ground,
a place to meet, to lay weapons aside.
The pulse of a passing native sound
uses tarab to start the tide
in a surge of Siberian blood.
A man's graveled throat cause a cascade
as jazz melds tradition. In contrast,
drumming or hitting strings then flood
the swelling lilt of sirens' serenade
that bonds now to a mysterious tribal past.

First published in *Writing World: World Music Day*

WORDS FROM A WOMAN ALIVE
(ode for Ana Elizabeth Cintron-Diaz)

Incisions are cut so close to the heart,
it's as if that organ itself was amputated
as bandages cover a body torn apart
hide the trench of a breast excavated,
now a valley of scar tissue and pain
where the agent of my gender
has been sliced by a surgeon's knife.
Drugs cannot completely constrain
the cancer demanding my surrender,
but I refuse the disease the trophy of my life.

First published in *The Power of the Feminine I*, vol. 2

A FERLINGHETTI OVILLEJO

He came forth from the sequoia—
and like Goya,
he bridged commonplace with regal.
He saw people,
noting the events of his age
using the page
as witness to human outrage.
Lawrence, a modern Emerson
for his, the Beat generation,
and like Goya, he saw people using the page.

First appeared in *Memorial Poetry*

VILLANELLE SANS LIBERTÉ

Welcome to the collective hive,
the M.C. from the center ring cries,
Where being numb means being alive!

Acrobats, jugglers, and clowns arrive
with no festive feel—as everyone sighs,
"Welcome to the collective hive."

The crowd below climbs the high dive
grateful to lunge to their own demise
where being numb means being alive.

Individuals could not survive
from consuming the ringmaster's lies.
Welcome to the collective hive

where personalities cease to strive;
defeat is transmitted through their eyes—
where being numb means being alive.

Spirit has died; there's no more drive,
and true liberty lost all allies.
Welcome to the collective hive
where being numb means being alive.

First published in *Villanelles: Four Feathers*

CIGARETTE SENRYU

Defying the rules
holding against convention
the last smoker stands

CLIMBER'S SENRYU
(for tree surgeons, roofers, line workers, among others)

Heights have the highest
respect for those of us who
respect them in turn.

MULLET SENRYU

The mullet returns.
Is this the best we can do
to comb up the past?

First appeared in *Fine Lines*

SIJO FOR DIANNE SCHURR

Her body waxes and wanes like the moon, but her honeyed voice
remains true, mercurial in range, constant in sustain.
The world, living within her, sounds of beauty without sight.

First appeared in *Startled by Music*

THE ARTIST'S SIJO

If it's true, Vincent Van Gogh heard 47 voices within his head,
then gathered them to spill colors on canvas in swirls and shapes.
He saved us from sacrificing our own ears to the knife.

First appeared in *Body Parts: Four Feathers*

MY SHAKESPEARIAN MANIFESTO

Everyone else does it, so why not me?
Let me spill black ink on page upon page
with my twisted testimony, my creed,
a manifesto to dispense my rage.
Everyone has an origin story,
mine comes from deep in the cave of Plato,
and while I may live in allegory,
these pictures of life will fade to shadow.
In fevered dreams, I am heterodox
so have no need to decide on my prey.
I like to liken myself to Guy Fawkes,
but I'm more like Kaczynski or McVeigh.
To my successors, I leave human chum;
revolution serves as my opium.

THE STATE OF FLORIDA

Power ties gleam, Republican   red,
        men in suits crowding, taking the
        entire sidewalk, lemmings crossing
        the street, over the street. Autumn
        in Florida, a nip in the air and
        transients on the beach. "Rock Stars"
      touch a   flame to an aluminum
          can,   like the altar boys
            they once were. In
                truck cabs, nightsticks
                  rest in gun racks, a
                  window sticker says,
                  "If you ain't from Dixie,
                   You ain't shit," raising
                  the question: If I am from
                  Dixie, does that make me
                  shit? All over are the signs
                    of Southern hospitality
                    at its best: pit bulls and
                    beer cans in yards; stars
                   and bars fly above
                  cinderblock houses or
                  trailer homes mounted on
                      cinderblocks; a rusted
                      pick-up truck on the same;
                      crosses on   front
                      lawns—   burnt
                       offerings   to
                       the gods   of
                          small-minded
                       racism. All
                          this,
                         and
                      hot Fall
                  weather
         too.

First appeared in *Top 30 Bards of Southern California*

THE DREAM-STATE SELF
Imaginings, either good or bad

WHERE ARE THE DRAGONS WHEN WE NEED THEM?

We dip oars into waters of delicate daring,
stroke to the universal pulse, use echolocation
to slouch our way into the New Stone Age, burning
coals of devotion. In uncertain generations,

what comes next? Desertion is allowed but not feasible
when the planet's too small to escape. Calamities can
make demons weep like he whose name must not be said
or Lazarus being raised from the dead.

History is read in linear fashion; reality
rarely goes so. Poisonous thorns of a stone rose
prick the chronic euphoria of Pollyanna Syndrome,
bleeding into sumptuous joy of brutality.

First appeared in *Line of Poetry*

INVERTED ANNIVERSARY

Boarding, bags packed with miseries,
the couple tries to return to talk.

They work between the burning
of each other's pain to escape

the churning shadows of their origins:
his father's tantrums, her mother's martyrdom.

Last night they touched as they slept in the bed
they share separately. She kicked his leg away

rather than retreat; they even skirmish in sleep.
Fulfilling their ration of disdain,

they've approached apology,
wanting to restore love but

can barely even muster anger,
preferring to wallow in the numb.

A NEW METROPOLIS

How do I pack for the upcoming end times?

The burger joint's sign instructs,
"Skip the straw—it's the law!"
Tantalizing entreaties to lead the citizenry
into accepting oppression.
Beware the spores that invade
and induce you to take the pledge.

I abhor A.I. because
I fear learning something
about myself
I don't want to know.

Then,
I dread the feedback loop
of high-speed processors and video screens with
supercalifragilisticexpialahighdef,
swallowing people into the bowels of science
as if that can cure all ills.

Before Skynet injected
intelligence into the machines,
Fritz Lang gave us the catacombs,
where proles lived under the thumbs
of those above and used games
to dazzle, distract, and hypnotize.
The batteries are low and
need to be replaced.

World leaders gather to concur:
"Citizens should demur
from eating too much meat."
Adding "for the good of the planet"
as they carve into piles of prime rib.

Forget the peace dividend.
The fruits of war come from contracts.

Where is the blood
I can paint on the lintel
when the lunatic
we put at the head of the table
puts it all into focus, screaming
"You ain't seen nuttin' yet."

LET'S ALL GET DOWN AND DO THE LOWEST COMMON DENOMINATOR

I see my past self
sitting on a porch with
a carton of Luckies
and a brown quart bottle of
the one beer to have when
having more than one.

In the distance, two falcons nest
under an overpass
of the Northern State Parkway;
the road brings drivers to Jericho
and miles of merchandise.

Shopping malls are
caricatures of our way of life;
what one learns in these places about
our true nature will keep anthropologists
in stitches for hours.
A bookstore displays a tome emblazoned
with basic black lettering against a solid white cover that reads
        "No Frills Romance,
        complete with everything:
        A kiss, a promise, a
        misunderstanding, another kiss,
        a happy ending."
Just what we need in this age
of instantaneous gratification:
more generic sex.

Now we're lassoed, hog-tied, and branded
as we move along the new
digital trail, driven
by the algorithm.

First appeared in *Blooming Verses*

FEVER DREAM

Your grandfather's cult
didn't work; few ever do.

If I cannot earn trust,
allow me at least to achieve lust.

In my nightmare walks
down Vicodin Street,

I endure benadryl visions
where racial supremacysts fester

and kiss Roobha, who dances,
balanced between two worlds.

Forget Big Brother;
forget Big Business;

forget Big Whatever. Big Data
threatens more of us now.

First appeared in *Dreams: Four Feathers*

CATCHING THE WORLD IN COLLAGE
WITH A 35 MM SLR

A puppy peers through the gap between
a patio door and its frame.
He spies two owls, perhaps

mother and daughter? They stand
at the curb waiting for the light
to turn green and let them

cross the street in safety. Meanwhile,
behind the Pomeranian,
in the library, Eli

stands looking up at the top
shelf, waiting to be able
to reach high enough

to learn what others know.
Seeing that the coast is clear,
the pup plans his escape.

CREATED HATE

When action no longer counts,
some need to stand out,
to validate ourselves
by faking hate. The latest variation
of Munchausen involves the privilege of being
a victim: the new narcissism and a pathway to virtue.

Carnival barkers willing to Nifong dissent,
their priority becomes to drive
a woeful narrative to dilute reality
and hide behind "a greater truth."

So another cries, "I was attacked
          for my race
          or my gender
          or my faith."
Choose one from above, or insert
the category to your liking or use academispeak:
stick an X at the end of any word
and assume the mantle of Academx

Feel free to claim a plethora of pronouns
in a bountiful harvest of potential prejudice.
There is power in saying you've been
Smolletted by the Brawley Effect,
using slashed tires on cars painted with insulting epitaphs
or seeing nooses all around us
in a vile strain that strains genuine sympathy.

It's hard to be outraged
when so much is tagged
some desired form of hatred. After all, there has to be
suffering humanity.

All this leads me to doubt and wait
for reality to seep out, bubble up.

ENDTIMES BLUES

There is no Appomattox
during the apocalypse.
The worst of brutalities
become the norm—
are neither crimes nor
even
sins.

People devour one another
as a matter of routine
and inevitability.
She shrugs—once—
and then
digs
in.

WHEN "YES" ISN'T ENOUGH

People insist their land is always holiest,
their place of origin the most perfect
even as they run from it as fast as they can,
but I can never escape when I come from,
surrounded by leaders who talk like Churchill
but behave like Chamberlin. Political
speech is synthetic and artificial; it thrives
in the Kingdom of the Hyperbolic.

The world is mannequin-clown scary. As brains fail,
I can almost see it: the synapses flail,
reaching out—anywhere, trying to find any
thought that momentarily had just been there—
perhaps hiding in a corner of my mind
or—just as likely—gone for good. I'm an escapee
from images, memories, names, or thoughts that
become a congregation of vapors.

A LIFE ETCHED IN WALLS
(dedicated to Dumas and Dorsey)

Accused as a traitor to appease a rival's envy,
Edmond spent 30 years behind bars and walls away
from society, stranded *in communicado.*

Disallowed parchment or instrument, he fashioned
grey mortar into a blotter while a rock, broken
from the door frame, served as quill. In isolation,

he reshaped himself into a solitary scribe,
transcending the claustrophobic cell to assume life
outside the barricades of iron bars and spikes.

In time, he learned of the tunnels, connecting him
to the priest who taught him Scripture and logic. Meanwhile,
he conjured hatred and vengeance until he found

a way to replace his mentor's carcass to escape
the grim tower, diving into water, disguised
as his mentor's corpse to retrieve treasure,

later returning disguised to exact his revenge.
Edmond completes his story and fulfills his destiny,
weathering life to his own detriment.

First appeared in *All Your Poems*

THE BRAVERY OF MERCEDES
(from *Pan's Labyrinth*)

She slices the captain's cheek
from tragus to lip
with a willingness and skill
she gleaned from gutting pigs.

Her courage makes me want
to see how she saw,
feel what she felt,
but to do that

I'd have to endure the anguish
she suffered, watching a man
take joy in torture, slaughter
the innocents she tried to save.

Conscience rests on my chest
like a concrete pillow.
I feel the tickle of guilt
at the base of my neck,

like a guillotine blade
that cleaves my throat
and severs my head
from its body.

First appeared in *Line of Poetry*

Bill Cushing

WARNING LABELS

Our lives have become
less than an asterisk.

In uncertain times, what comes next?

Now our dangers are the fires in the brain
burning out who we are.

Rather than run the risk
of unhappiness,
let's get products that
work like magic, but
do not take if allergic.

Two tablets daily will keep you alert,
let you lose weight at the hips,
achieve smooth skin, full lips
with a slight risk of depression.

Side effects vary.

Contact your local physician in case of
thinning hair, vomiting,
discoloration of eyes or urine.

One application by hypodermic
reduces urges to urinate or masturbate,
dissolves kidney stones
although it may cause brittle bones
or a bit of rash.

Warning: this product may
cause dizziness, diarrhea, genital warts, or loosened jaw,
and there is the occasional dose of road rage,
perhaps infection
at the site of injection.

Clear clogged drains, toilets, and arteries
with the finest Egyptian cotton sheets.
Call now for a second free;
just pay handling fees.

Do not forget to use
the discount code
"fuxnoose."

First appeared in *Poetry Nook*

WHAT'S LEFT BEHIND HURTS MOST

Someone thumbtacked the moon too low
as well as off kilter tonight,
glimmering off the hermitage
she chose, wishing for the luck of
Thecla. She detected the patterns
before they could coalesce and
bloom into a sadistic scenario.
Now, sitting outside the A&P,
huddled in a cardboard box
like so many kittens or puppies,
squat the children she offers to give away.

First appeared in *Poet-Tree Imagazine*

TRYING TO BE NORMAL IN A ZOMBIE WORLD

Nice open wound you got yourself there
he declares, more for himself
than to anyone else.
It's not that he can't think;
it's that his zombie tongue refuses to work,
denies him the skill
to form the words
he tries to spit out,
like the bad brains he just ate.

In the abandoned haberdashery where he lives,
he hangs his bowler next to a pay phone,
decked in black and silver,
that stands sentry flanked by a calendar
and one yellowing, mildewed poster
that used to hold plastic pocket brushes,
some still glued to its surface.
Its vertical handpiece hangs
like a bulbous nose, lingering long.

Decaying sores create a connect-the-dots pattern
across our protagonist's back.
He wheezes even though
he no longer breathes. After all, trying to inhale—
a habit that lets him hold onto humanity—
proves difficult when dealing
with the sucking chest wound
left from one zombie-
hunter's errant shot.

First appeared in *Body Parts: Four Feathers*

TO SMITHEREENS

Humanity has become as fragmented as
a Braque painting or the sound of Tojo singing
the banzai blues. Living by euphemisms,
there seems to be a sale on cliches today.

I live within an Escher woodcut where
linear perspective is fragmented, explodes
as nuns float above the pews singing
"Nearer, my Lord, to thee."

Commonplace events remind me of uncommon
occurrences while a pride of laughing lions,
embedded in embroidery, peer at me.
The world may look whole from a distance,

but viewed closer, I see the rusted pipes
or rotting tiles on a roof forming
dots of color that might have fallen from
a bombardment by Marshal Zhukov.

First appeared in *Last Stanza Poetry Journal*

BREAD AND CIRCUSES, STREAMING AT 9 EASTERN

Gil Scott was right: the revolution won't be televised.
Wars will.
Conflict gets its own deal.
Nothing can be improvised
in this, our new industry.
The bureaucratic beast demands bones to grind
into meal for its feast.

Forget flak jackets;
we need more publicity flacks,
alchemists of propaganda,
hacks who turn tragedy into inspiration.
We'll prop the heroes we create, then present them
to the nation
as adjectives like "honor" and "courage" cascade

while we blind the public with parades.
Let there be no doubt—they'll shovel the shit
faster than truth can ooze out.
Just make sure no eyes
get a chance to spy
coffins
unloaded from cargo planes.

THE LAST LOGO ON EARTH

Once we run out of cars
to drop into the ocean
and mold into ersatz
coral reefs, what corporate symbol
will be left on land to serve
as the final sign of
manufacture? Perhaps
we'll leave this planet,
head for the border, desert our own ruins
to carve a sneaker's swoosh
on the moon
or loose satellites, set them
in swirling orbit to create
blinking lights that spell L-G:
"Life's Good."

First appeared in *Cathexis North*

SOUVENIRS

Waiting on the promised end times,
the erosion of age absorbs
but does not erase the remains.
They are out there all around us:

Skulls piled high by centurions;
blackened bodies, impressions
scorched into earth by flame throwers
of the Great War. Then,

glazed eyes gaze at the world from those
draped in aprons of skin and thrown
in wooden wagons like human
debris by soldiers of the Reich;

and wretched blood retched on sand
from biological weapons.
Feeling feral charm, men with clenched
fists and clenched minds descend

into woeful revenge, and passion
waxes as we join the westering sun,
and the heat of living flashes
and fades into desolation.

First appeared in *Neopoet*

AFTER *OVE*

The burial, prayers, and eulogies ended,
he sits by the closet where her clothes hang suspended.

He strokes the woolen sleeve of her favored coat,
holds it up, cups it to his face, and dotes

on the last traces of her perfume knowing she
was his bliss and proclaims, "You were to outlive me."

Tears erupt as her voice travels through his head,
and he mulls joining her among the dead.

First appeared in *Poet-Tree Imagazine*

TWO BROTHERS RETURN HOME

Stopping along the edge of a road now neglected,
they peer down at the decaying carcass of
what pretended to be home. The pitched roof sags
under the invisible weight of the past.
What windows have not been broken by thrown stones
are coated with the grime of neglect.
Planks of its walls fall, as if the rot of the past,
the years of abuse, had leeched out.

"You should forgive Da," the older pleads.
It's his last request as he's wheeled over the threshold
into the collapsing interior, now about to become
a place of death for his own dying body
that disintegrates, becoming useless,
going down its own hill. He welcomes
the piercing needle that will let him become
one more memory of this place.

The younger brother leaves, his task complete.
Plodding back to his spot on the road,
he ponders his brother's petition. He allows
tears to flow—enough, perhaps, to cleanse his bile
but not near enough to douse the tongues of fire
that now lick the walls and become sheets of flame that
shroud this shell of the past, turning what remains
of a child's hell into ash.

DRENÂND SÂNGELE VIETII*

Lingering within Corvin castle's aging ramparts,
vampiric images fill doorways, invade hearts
in dreams to seek shade beneath carnivorous plants.
The corroded metallic smell of rancid blood
clogs nostrils with the flaking and chalky motes of grout.
The building decays into ruin, not unlike its owner.
A dread storm arises, escapes the repugnant
residue of light into gloom, the *empusa* beguiles
from within the murk through the power of *basso sonant*.
To gain refuge from the light, stepping into a dark
more dangerous than Orlok's shadow, it cannot conceal
the pus of eras that bleeds from scabbed and rotting skin.
This partner to pestilence never mutes the slurp and slosh
of feeding as it mounts each victim's breast, growling
from shadows, assuring them, "I am appetite, not the eater."

First appeared in *Shadows: Four Feathers*

*Romanian for "Draining the blood of life"

RESTRAINING THE BEAST WITHIN

Crouching within my cranium,
its curved spine crammed inside
my skull, having grown out of my
reptilian complex, tethered
to a binary plane where
thinking is *ancien regime.*
Its fangs align with my nostrils
as if those flared voids might provide
hatches to make its escape.
Its left hand, claws out, pushes down
and against my chin, perhaps
trying to create a portal
from my mouth. Its arms clog my ears,
diminishes the low hum
of others' invading voices.
Reason tries to disrupt my life,
infuses calm to try and restrain
the brute residing in the brain
with a Windsor knot of virtue.

First appeared in *Portal Poetry*

Bill Cushing

Meet the Author

Raised in New York, Bill Cushing lived in numerous states, the Virgin Islands, and Puerto Rico. Returning to college later in life, he was called the "blue collar poet" by peers at the University of Central Florida because of his time serving in the Navy and working as a marine electrician—among other jobs—for several years thereafter. He earned an MFA in writing from Goddard College in Vermont.

He now resides in Glendale, California with his wife and their son. He recently retired after more than 20 years teaching in Los Angeles area colleges but continues teaching part time. Bill has four previous poetry collections: *A Former Life, Music Speaks*, "*. . .this just in. . .*", and *Just a Little Cage of Bone.*

He has also written a short story collection (*The Commies Come to Waterton*) and two books of creative non-fiction including *Heroic Brothers of the Civil War.*

Bill can be contacted at piscespoet@yahoo.com
His website address is https://www.mywriteronline.net/

Previous Works

POETRY

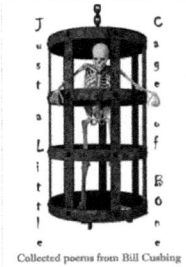

Just a Little Cage of Bone
https://www.amazon.com/dp/1960038109

2024 American Writing Award (Finalist)

. . .this just in. . .
https://www.amazon.com/this-just/dp/8182537460/

Music Speaks
https://www.amazon.com/Music-Speaks-Bill-Cushing/dp/0359827012/

2019 Gabriel Valley Poetry Festival winning chapbook
2023 New York City Book Award (Bronze)

A Former Life
https://www.amazon.com/Former-Life-Bill-Cushing/dp/1635349389/

2019 Kops-Fetherling International Award

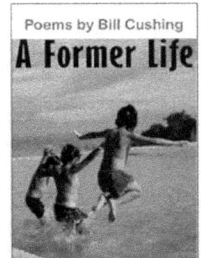

CREATIVE NON-FICTION

Time Well Spent
https://www.amazon.com/dp/196003846X

Heroic Brothers of the Civil War
https://www.amazon.com/
Heroic-Brothers-Civil-Bill-
Cushing/dp/1960038478

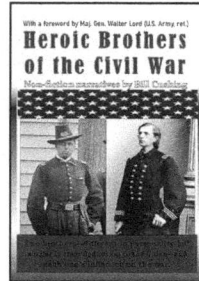

2024 Global Literary Book
Award (Historic Nonfiction)

FICTION/SHORT STORIES

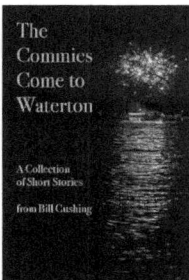

The Commies Come to Waterton
https://www.amazon.com/Commies-Come-
Waterton-Bill-Cushing/dp/8119228200/

www.ingramcontent.com/pod-product-compliance
Lightning Source LLC
Chambersburg PA
CBHW071816020426
42331CB00007B/1503